Oliver Cromwell

CROMWELL: LORD OF THE FENS

ISBN 0 901680 85 0

Published by T. Bevis BA, 28 St. Peter's Road, March, Cambs. PE15 9NA
(Tel: 01354 657286)

Printed by David J. Richards Ltd., Printers and Stationers, 1 West Park Street, Chatteris, Cambs. PE16 6AH (Tel: 01354 692947) (Fax: 01354 692299)

INTRODUCTION

Oliver Cromwell, a middle-class farmer, restructured democracy, founded the Commonwealth and was architect of British sea power and the modern army. A practical joker and ardent Puritan, Cromwell enjoyed drinking with friends and dull and dour he certainly was not. He experienced financial difficulties in his early life and always his youthful times as a mischievous boy remained with him. He underwent a momentous change and experienced a dramatic religious conversion, inspiring him to write: "Oh, I have lived in and loved darkness and hated the light. I was a chief, the chief of sin-ness; I hated Godliness, yet God had mercy upon me. Oh, the richness of His mercy." Cromwell believed that Charles the First who enveloped himself with elaborate Catholic rituals and much influenced by the Queen was against the British Reformation. He was concerned that Roman Catholic Europe would one day launch an attack against Protestant England. Cromwell believed that England must be strong and could not afford in his time a King who had married a woman who consistently influenced her husband. He rose to Second-in-Command of the army during the Civil War, Sir Thomas Fairfax, Lord General of the army in overall command. Cromwell, Lieutenant General of Horse commanded the army at the Battle of Naseby, a defining action in the conflict between Parliament and Royalists.

An exceptional leader Cromwell took risks. Amazingly, he had never received military training yet he proved to be an outstanding commander and excelled as a cavalry officer. He was a masterful military and political tactician. Cromwell's disciplined "Ironside" soldiers were renowned for their tactical ability and for carrying the fight forward and victoriously without any fear. The infantry men were Britain's first red-coat soldiers. Officers were middle-class yeomen initially drawn from the Fens and Cromwell called them "lovely company, honest Christian soldiers" and they fought spiritedly. The King's Cavaliers never beat them. Cromwell was a champion for religious liberty and in his time there was more freedom of conscience than at any other time in English history. When the last battle had been fought Cromwell believed it was still necessary for the country to have a King, but on a constitutional basis. He attempted to persuade the King to re-occupy the throne on constitutional terms, such as we enjoy now. King Charles, aided and abetted by the Queen, harboured other plans and it was inevitable that Cromwell and his Parliamentary committee had no choice but have him executed. Oliver Cromwell set our land on course to greatness and international respect. He was aware of his own flaws, but never has England seen a man of his calibre. An all-rounder he was England's Man Of Action and he occupies the highest pinnacle in Britain's remarkable history. Born on the edge of the Fens, Cromwell loved the huge expanse of wetlands with its protruding islands and stoical inhabitants and he declared he would fill the Isle of Ely with a godly people and it would become a place fit for God to dwell in. Oliver Cromwell was truly self-styled Lord of the Fens.

Cromwell : Lord of the Fens

The Civil War was the greatest tragedy to inflict our nation. Wars of this nature brings out the worst in men. Civil war is invariably spawned by oppression from the highest places ensconced in hereditary right and nearly always there emerges in a cloak of insignificance a champion destined to guide his stricken country to a haven of security, strength and respect from the murky depths of oppression, frustration and unfairness.

He that is born for the part of liberating a nation is forever associated with the elevation of his country from the quagmire of spiritual and political regression to a pinnacle of impressive height, even though the horror of war be deemed unavoidable and necessary. That man was Oliver Cromwell, a Fenman by adoption. It was written of him *"He may have been regarded as a traitor to his King, but never to his country."* The author is emboldened to suggest Oliver Cromwell and Winston Churchill were the greatest men born for the purpose of saving our country from the greed of kings and nobility and in another age saving it from the march of Fascism, thus elevating it to a pinnacle of respect.

Cromwell was born at Huntingdon on the edge of the Fens. We can walk along the street that he knew and see opposite the market place All Saints' church where his parents brought him to be baptised in 1599. We may also see the school he attended as a young boy. It is one of the oldest buildings in the country, erected by the Normans and, in our own times appropriately used as the Cromwell Museum. It contains several artifacts and personal belongings of the man himself.

When he was a vexatious young lad who then would have thought he would one day become a troublesome spirit to Royalists, and that this spirit would be fanned into a flame igniting common people's awareness that it was unacceptable for kings to govern wrong. Royal mismanagement of the country added fuel to ordinary mens resentment of royal prerogative. This sparked the revolt led by Puritans.

Milton wrote of Cromwell "the Chief of Men," a man of extraordinary vision, courage and action; none other like him. Cromwell, self-styled Lord of the Fens, grew to love the vast area of undrained Fenland and admired the stoical attitudes of the inhabitants who had learned to grapple with nature in her worst moods. His birth heralded imminent changes to the royal prerogative of ruling the country which shook the English throne to its foundations. The history of the Civil War has passed down to our times and is no less stirring as in Cromwell's time. His father lies in All Saints' church, Huntingdon, and his devoted, careful mother was taken by her son to the adorned chapel of Henry the Seventh at Westminster for burial. Her stay there was brief. In the reign of Charles the Second her remains were irreligiously exhumed and cast into a pit.

The young Oliver was the bane of his neighbours and terrorised them. Like another young Fenman, the famous Hereward who kept William The Conqueror at bay from the Fens, he lived a wild life but all that changed on reaching a mature age. Cromwell's father and his wealthy uncle at Hinchingbrooke were unhappy about him, but his mother gently persuaded him to abandon his wild ways and study seriously at school, later studying at Sidney Sussex college, Cambridge. The Huntingdon school Oliver attended despite its great age is still intact. It has a lovely Norman entrance through which he entered. It originally served as the hall of the Norman hospital and without any doubt its most famous pupils were the two friends, Oliver Cromwell and Samuel Pepys. At the Restoration of the Monarchy in 1660 Pepys penned he was mortified to see the head of England's man of action impaled on a spike at Westminster. It was, he wrote, an indignity for so great a man.

Cromwell's first lessons were under the supervision of a Huntingdon minister, Dr. Beard, who instructed him at the grammar school. Oliver was much in the mould of other young lads, alternately studying hard then playing truant for a month or so! He said he once had a vision of a huge figure opening the curtains of his bed, telling him he would become the greatest person in the kingdom. A prophetic vision indeed, for that is what he became and he changed the historical course of the country.

Surprisingly and wrongly there is no distinctive monument to Huntingdon's greatest son although there is a plaque fixed near the school's doorway. It was left to St. Ives, nearby, to do him the single honour of erecting a very impressive sculpture of the great man in the town's market place, typically with bible in one hand and sword dangling from a belt. Suppression burdened the country and prompted Cromwell to consider emigrating. He almost sold his land in preparation to sail away from England to escape Laud's persecution, but changed his mind. The country was in a rebellious mood and Civil War loomed on the horizon. Cromwell, then MP for Cambridge acted to prevent the king from taking control of armed trained bands, a force recruited among the commoners. The Civil War proved Cromwell's strategical worth measured not only in military but in political terms. Scornful of the king's cavalier manner surrounded by a swashbuckling assembly of feather-hatted warriors drawn generally from the nobility, the army Royalists to a man but largely devoid of strategical planning adhered to the old practice of meeting the enemy head-on, Cromwell realised radical changes were necessary for future military planning and initially gathered recruits from the Fens, subjecting them to rigorous, disciplined and strategical manoeuvres hitherto unheard of in the military history of England or abroad. Motivated by the stalemate at Newbury he introduced new training methods and called the army the New Model. It set the ideal for modern armies worldwide and was England's first red coat army.

Cromwell led his men nicknamed Ironsides and Roundheads after the practical armour and helmets they wore with unwavering determination. His army of foot and especially the New Model cavalry swept all before them. Cromwell's Puritan battalions gained a reputation for valour and tactical deployment on the battlefield and the enemy, valorous as they were, had no real answer. The battles of Naseby, Marston Moor, Worcester and Dunbar among others were major triumphs for Cromwell and heralded the eventual downfall of the king and his unacceptable ways of meddling with Parliament. An outstanding horseman, a siege master, a world class cavalry leader, Cromwell, Lord of the Fens, was a supreme strategist and tactician. He subdued any that argued against principled government and acted as a hammer against any representing the old ways of governing the country and who supported Royalist domination.

Cromwell overran Wales and Scotland. Nothing could withstand his military prowess. Nevertheless he recognised that future kings, albeit as figureheads, could serve a useful purpose in uniting the country. When the final battle of the Civil War has been fought it was his wish to restore Charles the First to the throne on a legal constitutional basis. The King, however, had other ideas and wrote a letter to the Queen in France which was intercepted by Parliament, intimating he would use Cromwell for as long as necessary then hang him. That was the catalyst for Charles' downfall. It was really his fault that fate awaited him at the hands of the axeman. At the end of the day it was "my life or thine." If Charles had not sought to restore the suppressive form of royal prerogative and its biased leanings upon Parliament he could well have continued the role of sovereign under constitutional conditions such as we enjoy now.

Cromwell's action in Ireland, particularly at Drogheda in 1649 sullied his reputation over the centuries. In that sanguinary conflict he took account of the Royalists' refusal to surrender and they received help from citizens. It brought out a stern Puritanical reaction to contain what was becoming a crisis. Cromwell's forces gave no quarter. At heart Cromwell favoured tolerence and freedom of conscience. He criticised Presbyterians and other independent sects who searched for Baptists and hanged them. After the beheading of King Charles Cromwell was invited to become king but he declined and accepted the title of Lord Protector instead. In this role he carried out his desire to give the country freedom of worship and meaningful law and order with strict penalties for any that offended. The Anglican Church was overwhelmingly Royalist and this vexed him. In his view the Church had to be controlled and encouraged to practice its faith on simple, less dogmatic lines.

Cromwell's New Model Army was not merely victorious over its enemies in Britain it spoke volumes of the nation's powerful role in military expediency and political might. Europe looked on with a sense of awe and the New Model conducted successful, tactical campaigns abroad. Through the army's efforts Cromwell influenced Portugal, Sweden, Holland and Denmark. France and Spain seeing the invincibility of the man competed for an alliance with Parliament. The English fleet, an impressively strong maritime force, became ruler of the seas and Jamaica was added to England's foreign possessions. Puritan England possessed the most efficient military power in the world. Holland challenged it and Dutch Admiral van Tromp declared he would sweep the English from the seas and carried a broom on the prow of his flagship to emphasise his boast. Admiral Blake commander of the English fleet engaged the Dutch fleet off Portland Bill, Dorset and almost annihilated it, many of the Dutch men-o'-war ending up on the sea bed. Hundreds of Dutch sailors were marched to the Fens and set to work cutting out the New Bedford Level drain which had been designed by Sir Cornelius Vermuyden a Dutchman, while Scottish prisoners-of-war worked on the same drain from the opposite direction.

Oliver Cromwell was not a humourless, miserable person usually associated with the Puritan way of thinking. He displayed a contagious sense of humour, enjoyed intellectual company, was fond of music and art and attended races. He was conversely familiar with the bible and understood human ways. Cromwell was tolerant of most things but were he severely provoked he gave vent to great anger. He was inwardly and outwardly strong, with determined features and, aware of any lack of beauty in himself, asked the artist to paint him "wart and all." It was written of him: "Though God made him a heart wherein there was little room for any fear but what was due himself of what was a large portion, yet did he exceed in tenderness towards sufferers. A large soul . . . has seldom dwelt in a house of clay than his was."

Staunch Royalists never allowed the failings of the King to impinge upon their senses. They regarded Cromwell, the mightiest of Puritans, as a man possessed of the devil. When Cromwell put aside the plough and wielded the sword he cleaved a passage through the hollows of despair and oppression burdening the citizens of a nation chronically sick at heart. It thrust deep into the bowels of royal prerogative whereby, for centuries, kings and queens had squandered their fortunes on war and high living, on extravagances the country could ill afford. At the end of it all when the king had been disposed of through his own intransigence, Cromwell wrote: "He that ventures his life for the liberty of his country, I wish trust God for the liberty of his conscience and for the liberty he fights for."

Even now, more than 300 years later, people align themselves with either the Royalist or Parliamentary cause. Brave deeds motivated by cherished principles live on. Stirring stories emerge from gory fields of battle illuminating it seems for ever elevated individuals standing among the flamboyant ranks of nobility and their swashbuckling sons and the severe, principled and disciplined young warriors of the New Model Army raised from the freeborn farmers of the wet flatlands of Cambridgeshire of which Oliver Cromwell was one.

Huntingdon's famous son (infamous some would have it) was once recalled to mind by a citizen of St. Ives as a young man wearing a piece of red flannel beneath his chin as he walked to church on Sundays. Years later he was remembered as an extraordinary leader who had shaken an erring monarchy corrupt through and through, who rebuilt those crumbling foundations and in the process revitalised the country's system of government restoring the nation to a standing never before known.

Oliver Cromwell received estates at Ely through the bequest of his uncle, Sir Thomas Steward, who died in 1636. Thus Cromwell departed from St. Ives where he and his family including his widowed mother lived and took up residence at Ely's charming old Glebe House opposite the cathedral. It was there in the charming old house now used as Ely's Tourism Centre that Cromwell succeeded to the office of Farmer of the Tithes. This enabled him to take a keen, hard look at the industrious, if coarse, Fen people and he liked what he saw. The Fens had always fascinated him, its stoical history reflecting to some extent his own attitudes. In later years when peace had returned to the land, a former Royalist opponent wrote of Cromwell's high regard for the Isle of Ely: "Colonel Cromwell told me he would make the Isle of Ely the strongest place in the world and he would make it a place fit for God to dwell in . . ."

It was while resting at Ely with his family during a lull in the Civil War Cromwell, then Governor of the Isle, brought his eyes to bear on ceremonial services which continued to take place in the cathedral. He addressed the Reverend Hitch, precentor, ordering him to "forebear from the unedifying and offensive ceremony lest the soldiers should in any tumultuous or disorderly way attempt the reformation of the cathedral."

Mr. Hitch took no notice and continued his dialogue from the pulpit, and Cromwell with a detachment of soldiers to hand approached the clergyman for a second time. Wearing his hat, Cromwell ordered the reverend to come down and dismiss the congregation. The precentor paused and continued as before. In adamant manner again Cromwell ordered him to come down and "stop fooling." This led to the cathedral being closed indefinitely. The Lord of the Fens re- action towards what he considered was unsavoury ways of conducting worship made him enemies. He was never overawed by church buildings and apparel worn by clergy and even less did he tolerate ritual and superstitious dogma. It is true that some churches did suffer at the hands of Parliamentary soldiers, but in the main troops were ordered to practice restraint and act orderly at all times. Royalist troops were not much better and seized any building to resist the Ironsides. Both sides looted shops and private homes; Cromwell himself ordered that all property and goods should be respected. It is known he ordered a soldier to pay for goods which had been taken from a shop.

The Parliamentary cause drew its strength from East Anglia and the Fens which by and large escaped the tumult and bloodiness of the Civil War. The Association was the only organisation at the time possessing the requisite elements of permanence. Due to its geographical location to the west and north of East Anglia and bordering with Lincolnshire and Northants where Royalists were active, the Isle of Ely naturally protected by marsh and meres formed a protective bastion against the royal army and this was fundamentally important to Parliament. The Fens offered a protective flank against attack. The king realised its importance and Royalists explored the possibility of entering the Isle to wrest the region from Parliamentary control.

Fen inhabitants shared mixed feelings over events in which they were occasionally the centrepiece. Disturbances engineered by Royalist sympathisers at Ely and Wisbech were put down by Cromwell's men. At March, Whittlesey and Wisbech Royalists caused a few anxious moments and General Fairfax who had his headquarters at Colchester entertained grave doubts about the safety of the Isle of Ely. Realising the importance of the Isle he advised greater security in the Cambridgeshire Fens and encouraged "honest men to take up arms against the king where they can be found." Col. John Hobart of Outwell formed a troop of seventy horse stationed at the sconce, a fortified palisaded earthwork in the vicinity of St. Wendreda's church, March. This fortification was central to operations in the Cambridgeshire Fens. At the same time a military road was made between Mepal and Chatteris. It was named Ireton's Way after Cromwell's son-in-law, an achieved soldier, and allowed direct access to March. Another military road was cut between Westry, near March, and Whittlesey. The March based cavalry enjoyed speedy access to wherever their services were required including the small Parliamentary palisaded earthwork west of Whittlesey commanding the road from Peterborough into the Fens. They also used the road north of March to Wisbech where a small garrison of Ironsides kept their eyes on the highway from Lincolnshire towards Wisbech. The sconce at March was excavated in the 19th century by a Captain Hamilton who discovered the skulls of several horses, military artifacts and clay pipes presumably used by the garrison. He also discovered large blocks of stone in the middle of the earthworks suggesting that a building had stood there which was probably used by the garrison, and also clues suggesting that a drawbridge stood on the site. The building, probably medieval, may have been the original Eastwood Manor.

Royalist troops under the command of Prince Rupert assembled in Lincolnshire and caused anxious moments among the Isle defenders but the King's men were probably put off making a determined effort to enter the Isle of Ely by the nature of the environment, marsh and fen, known to have sucked boats and their occupants into the mud never to be seen again, except centuries later when farmers' ploughs brought to the light of day mummified bodies of people who were caught seemingly unaware of the dangers when fog descended upon them and the sun went down and, disorientated, they too went down.

Colonel Watson in overall charge of the Isle's military emplacements, knew of places in the Fens which harboured Royalist sympathisers, especially at Wisbech. If the Royalists were to have any success of commanding the Isle of Ely they first had to secure Wisbech and March. Both Parliament and Royalists viewed Wisbech as a key town and if the King's men had taken the old borough they would have gained access to any part of the Isle and opened a front against the Eastern Counties Association. As it was the Marquis of Newcastle with a formidable army marched daily towards the Fens. Cromwell successfully besieged King's Lynn thereby gaining command of the highway from Spalding to Lynn. All roads into the Fens were under Parliamentary observation.

When King's Lynn was being besieged some Wisbech citizens given to gossiping, were heard talking about Captain Dobson who had his headquarters in the town. The Reverend Lee, Rector of Newton, and a Mr. Wilson were joined by John Richie an apothecary who watched the Captain mounted upon

An old photograph of the building which began as the hall of the 12th century hospital. It became Huntingdon's grammar school attended by two boys Oliver Cromwell and Samuel Pepys who made their mark in the world. The building is now the Oliver Cromwell Museum and houses several items including his death mask and his hat.

Cromwell's house at Ely. While at Ely, Cromwell became Farmer of Tithes and lived with his large family at this attractive half-timbered building opposite Ely cathedral. It serves now as the local Tourism Information Centre. Several of its rooms can be entered, for instance Mrs. Cromwell's kitchen and a haunted bedroom.

Cromwell walked through this entrance at Ely Cathedral and ordered the Precentor to "stop fooling".

his horse and remarked "Look! Yonder comes that rogue Dobson. I could find it in my heart to knock his brains out; he will never be killed else." Mr. Lee bade him be patient awhile, "There was one (the Marquis) coming, a doctor, who would let them all bleed in good time and he would do it to that purpose."

There were several Royalist sympathisers at Wisbech and Captain Dobson knew it. As the Marquis drew daily nearer to the Fens the captain ordered that all known Royalists in the town be rounded up, including Mr. Richie, and be locked in Wisbech parish church until the danger had passed. The prisoners held a daily ritual and held goblets of wine over the font while making the toast to "the King over the water" (Charles The Second in waiting). Another toast was to drop a bread crumb into the goblet of wine while saying "May divine providence send this crumb well (Cromwell) down."

In the early stages of the siege at King's Lynn Oliver Cromwell personally directed operations against fairly stiff opposition. This was conducted from the west side of the River Ouse where he positioned cannon and considerable damage was caused to the town including St. Margaret's priory church. A local tradition exists relating to the time that Cromwell, en-route to Lynn with a large company of soldiers and horse via March, having reached Friday Bridge, the day far spent, stopped overnight at Needham Hall. He received a courteous welcome from the owner and was offered a comfortable bed. Cromwell told him his troop would be spending a cold night in stables and outhouses and since next day he himself would probably be spending the night in a field he could not therefore sleep in a comfortable warm bed but would rest on a table instead. The table survived at the hall for a few centuries. In 1827 there lived at the parish of Elm a man far advanced in years who recalled his grandfather telling him that he remembered a long column of Ironsides led by Cromwell going along the track to Needham Hall.

The Fens' greatest contribution to Parliament's successful campaign was the force of foot and horse whose fighting ability proved beyond compare. The Ironsides, God-fearing conscientious men, evolved from the russet-coated Fen yeomen, a hardy race descended from the Gwywas (water people) that frequented the Fens in Roman and Anglo-Saxon times. They were tough souls and had to be, coping with an abysmal perpetually moist environment and able to make light of the ague, a form of malaria, common in the Fens that frequently killed upland visitors, not that many came to the area if they could help it! Cromwell's method of recruitment and revolutionary training methods had an abiding influence upon them. The Ironsides replied with a resounding "No!" to the King's demands. At Cromwell's bidding they left the fields and took up muskets, swords and pikes provided by sponsors, families and friends and trained in a highly disciplined manner as a force superior to the Royal army. The New Model Army and New Model Cavalry formed the embryo of modern armies worldwide. The Cavaliers were no match for them.

Threatened by Royalists with a sweeping aside by a stiff broom, it was the Fenmen and their recruits that wielded a stiffer broom. Donning russet coats, body "ironside" armour and "roundhead" helmets and armed with the specially commissioned "Souldiers bible," the Parliamentary army rose en mass and gained decisive victories at Marston Moor, Naseby and Worcester among other places, applying their brand of strategic warfare and tactical skills with astonishing effect. Oliver Cromwell's troop, mainly cavalry, was adjudged the finest in existence. Nothing withstood it. At the beginning of the Civil War the first battle ended as a draw and Cromwell realised that a new disciplined, strategical way of fighting was necessary rather than the medieval confrontational way of waging war. Thus the New Model Army was conceived.

Cromwell and Parliament are criticised mainly for governing methods so often seen in the modern world when revolutions end in military administration. Cromwell himself was neither cruel not tyrannical by nature, and is usually condemned for his repressive attitude in Ireland, a situation where he was provoked into excessively rigorous retaliation. Parliament's system of government did have an affect upon culture and the arts and this contributed to a return to the old ways under a restored monarchy and the country slipped from its respected pedestal. A victorious army usually sets about determining policy and errors can and do occur, greatly influencing military sternness in civil orders. Add to that a rare brand of Puritan discipline, the medicine can be uncommonly bitter. Despite the Protectorate's shortcomings one acknowledges the power and effectiveness of the New Model army as the only effective power in a nation the lifeblood of which was being drained by a succession of Kings and Queens that had acted as governments unto themselves and who were ill-fitted to reign, being driven by acquisitiveness in gaining power to wage useless wars and acquire wealth to their own wasteful ends.

For most part the English Civil War and successful campaigns in Scotland was a proving ground for cavalry, a resemblance of modern-day tank warfare. In this Cromwell excelled. Small freeholders known as yeomen, weary of the King's incessant demands, were led in example by the world's foremost cavalry officer. Governing the country proved to be a task where Parliamentary policy adhered to the whims of military influence and could not equal its fighting ability on the battlefield. The Republic was an experiment which would not last.

The system would have led to utter chaos were it not for Cromwell's practical statesman's instinct, but for most part law and order prevailed. Penalties for disregarding the law were severe, the ascent being on discipline in all facets of society and it was that which inhabitants finally rejected. Military adroitness within government is not really a good thing and we have had ample proof of the consequences relating to military rule in the world in our own times. The Ironsides followed Cromwell to a man. They gave England the embryo of a modern army much emulated in the world, and developed the cult of professional soldiers. The Ironsides' invincibility on the battlefields cannot but be admired. However, in cultural terms the Parliamentary army earned the condemnation of friend and foe alike. The mantra of the New Model was centred on tactical discipline and victory. Whenever the Ironsides stood fast and inflicted defeat upon their enemies they sounded the liberty bell for unborn generations. Cromwell argued with justification it was intolerable for kings to govern wrong and only a constitutional monarchy was tolerable, a policy which applies to this day.

What did Cromwell think of his fighting Fenmen and others that flocked to join them in his well fought campaign? "I raised such men as had the fear of God before them and made some conscience of what they did. And from that day forward they were never beaten; but wherever they were engaged against the enemy they beat continually."

Devoted to his family, Oliver Cromwell was a great man and a brave one. As the nation's Lord Protector and self-styled Lord of the Fens he ruled the country with a firm hand. England of his day had need of a strong leader. Cromwell was honest and a good friend to all honest men, but a dangerous and relentless opponent to all who succoured injustice. He did not suffer fools gladly. A wise man, he realised that England needed the monarchy and unwittingly devised a constitutional method of ruling the nation by a succession of kings and queens. At the Restoration in 1660 the ascent of Charles the second, so-called Merry Monarch, signaled the nation to indulge once more in weak and immoral practices. If we would compare the real worth of Oliver Cromwell and his services to his country, examine his leadership with the reign of Charles the Second which escalated the country into immoral decline.

All But King In Name

Charles The First declared on the scaffold he died "as a martyr of the people." Truth is the people had been martyrs to him and his biased claim of a King's rights. Charles was a bad judge of martyrs. Soon after his execution the House of Lords, deemed useless and dangerous, was abolished and a Council of State appointed to run the country. It comprised of forty-one members of which five were peers.

At the time the army consisted of 40,000 men and it was a hard task to manage them. Oliver Cromwell had been appointed by Parliament to command the army in Ireland where, antagonised by revolution he took revenge and made terrible havoc notably during the siege of Drogheda where no quarter was given. This siege is usually the yardstick by which Cromwell, all but King in name, is judged with no consideration to Drogheda's Royalist garrison and sympathetic inhabitants which is hardly ever mentioned, the cause of his retribution upon the town. Cromwell's favourite term in military matters was "they were knocked on the head" and when putting that into effect no holds were barred. He adopted the same attitude in Scotland. After Ireland Cromwell went to Scotland with 16,000 soldiers to fight the Scottish men. The Scottish leaders were canny, knowing they were no match for the Ironsides and would be beaten in an open fight. They reasoned if they lay quiet in their trenches Cromwell's men would be driven out by hunger and be forced to go away. The scene was set at Dunbar.

Scottish priests wanted their soldiers to fight and decided to interfere with something they knew nothing about, preaching long sermons exhorting the soldiers to come out and do battle and that is what they did. Cromwell fell upon them instantly, killing 3,000 and taking 10,000 prisoners, several hundred of whom were brought to the Fens to help in the drainage work.

The Scottish Parliament proclaimed the Prince of Wales Charles the Second in exile across the sea. On the 1st of January 1651 the Scottish people rallied for him at Scone, but Oliver Cromwell got out of bed in time and went to work with such determination and energy getting behind the Royalist army and severing all connections with Scotland. All the Scottish army (the Northern Foot) could do was painstakingly march to Worcester where the mayor and gentry proclaimed the Prince of Wales Charles the Second. Cromwell came rapidly to Worcester and he and his redoubtable Ironsides, building bailey-type bridges to cross the river, so laid about them in the great battle which was fought there, they beat the Scottish men and all but destroyed the Royalist army, though for five hours the Northern Foot and the Royalists fought valiantly.

Ireland being now subdued and Scotland kept quite by numerous forts and soldiers put there by Cromwell the next arena of activity was out to sea. The Dutch fleet under Admiral Van Tromp challenged Admiral Blake who commanded half the number of ships compared to the Dutchman and sent them out to engage in battle. Blake attacked the Dutch ships immediately with a raging broadside and sent Van Tromp packing.

The Dutch came back in the autumn with seventy ships and again challenged Blake whose battle group was still only half as strong as that commanded by Van Tromp. The business was settled off Portland Bill with the destruction of several Dutch men-o'-war and twenty-three captured. About 500 prisoners-of-war from this epic sea battle were brought to the Fens and like the Scottish prisoners-of-war they were set to work cutting drains, building embankments and improving natural rivers in the Fens.

By this time parliament had become weak and dispirited and Cromwell had designs upon it. He told members: "You are no parliament. Bring them in, bring them in," and Ironsides entered the House and ushered the members out. The Speaker was walked out of the building. Cromwell ordered that the mace which he called the "fools bauble" used to signify parliament was in session be carried away. Then he left and locked the door. After this extraordinary proceeding a new Council of State was formed and Cromwell was offered the opportunity of becoming king. He gave it thought but declined and later considered the title of Lord Protector. On December 11th 1653 a great procession formed outside Oliver Cromwell's house and he came out in a black velvet suit and large boots, got into a coach and was taken to Westminster. There in the Court of Chancery he publicly accepted the title of Lord Protector of the English nation. The City sword was handed to him and the seal and other things usually handed to kings and queens.

Cromwell, whom the people called "Old Noll", made a speech lasting three hours in which he advised 500 parliamentary members what to do for the credit and happiness of the country. In electing the members neither the Royalists or the Catholics were to have any share. He dismissed the assembly by telling the members to go to work and discourage what he described as frantic preachers who overdid their services in calling him a villain and a tyrant. If they ignored him he simply closed their chapels. This happened at Ely.

There was not at that time in England or anywhere else a man so capable of governing the country as did Oliver Cromwell. He ruled with a firm hand and levied a preponderant tax on Royalists (but not until they had been caught plotting against his life). Cromwell governed wisely and as the times required. Foreign countries respected his system of authority and it could be said that some politicians in modern times would do well to take a leaf from his book and promote Britain as an independent power standing against immorality and also unseemly practices in parliament and in other facets of society. Cromwell would have none of that. He sent Admiral Blake, a man with the foresight and tactical expertise of Vice-admiral Lord Nelson, to the Mediterranean Sea to make the Duke of Tuscany pay £60,000 for injuries he had done to British subjects. Cromwell sent Blake to Algiers, Tunis and Tripoli to have every English ship and every Englishman delivered to him that had been taken by pirates in those parts. It became known throughout the world that Britain was governed by a man in earnest, an avid promoter of justice who would not allow the English name to be insulted or slighted anywhere. Modern politicians please note. Cromwell's exploits in the name of Britain was clear to the Spanish ambassador that English ships must be free to go wherever they would, and that English merchants must not be thrown into dungeons as had happened.

The "King Over The Water" Charles (later the Second) represented a worn medieval monarchy and had no scruples about plotting with anyone for Cromwell's life. Cromwell had eyes and ears everywhere; he needed to and had several sources of information his enemies little dreamt of. There was a chosen body of persons called the Sealed Knot who were in the closest and most secret confidence of Charles in exile abroad. Sir Richard Willis, one of the foremost of them, acting like a double agent, reported to Cromwell everything that passed among them and was paid £200 per year for his pains. Much more, of course, can be written about Britain's extraordinary Lord Protector who raised the country to a mightily respected source of influence in the world.

In August 1658 Oliver Cromwell's favourite daughter Elizabeth, who had lost her youngest son, lay gravely ill and his mind was sorely troubled. Her father was very kind and loving to them all, being a good father and a good husband. He went down to Hampton Court to see his ailing daughter and could hardly be induced to stir from her side. Although his religion had been of a gloomy nature, his disposition had always been cheerful. He was fond of music in his home and good humoured. He kept open table once a week for all officers of the army above the rank of captain and always had in his home a quiet, sensible dignity. He would joke with his guests and tell them to their embarrassment where they had last raised their glass in a toast to the "king over the water", recommending them to be more private in future!

Oliver Cromwell bore the weight of heavy state affairs and had gone in fear of his life. He suffered from gout and ague (the latter a Fen malady) and when the death of his daughter occurred he sank never to raise his head again. Cromwell died on September 3rd 1658, the anniversary of the great battle of Worcester which he had called his fortunate day. He was 60 years of age. The day before his death and at times delirious, he was heard to utter a very good prayer. The country mourned his death and even Royalists acknowledged he was a great man and had raised the nation to a high level of international respect. His son, Richard, succeeded him.

It is ever to our country's shame that shortly after the Restoration of the Monarchy in 1660 Cromwell's body with three others that had participated in signing the King's death warrant were taken up from their graves and stood up clothed in shrouds at the bar of the Old Bailey, London, to be sentenced for treason, a macabre proceeding. The bodies were carted to Tyburn and hanged on the gallows. Their heads were decapitated and impaled on spikes opposite Westminster Hall. The head of Cromwell, for many years kept in private ownership, was finally buried at his old college Sidney Sussex, Cambridge.

It was very soon realised that a new age had descended upon the country and the king "over the water" was welcomed back as Charles the Second. Bells rang, down came the arms of the Commonwealth and up went the Royal Arms instead. Out of the public purse £50,000 was paid to the King and £10,000 for his brother the Duke of Gloucester, and prayers were said for the Stuarts at all churches.

Thus England became "merry" again to the heights of extravagance which Cromwell was so much against. The new king set up an ignoble example, himself enraptured by immoral standards and his eye alighted upon more than one lady including the infamous Nell Gwyn. He declared that he was one of the greatest, the wisest and the most noblest of kings that ever shone. Parliament in the humblest manner decreed that he receive £1,200,000 a year and to settle upon him for life that old disputed tonnage and poundage that under Cromwell had been so bravely fought against. Thus the country began its descent into dereliction as it had under Charles the First, and Cromwell's head cut off from his corpse stuck on a spike overlooking the River Thames witnessed all that he had fought for and achieved disappear into the mists of history.

The Cromwells at Wicken

Wicken, a small village between Stretham and Soham, is justifiably famous for its popular unspoilt undrained fen, the National Trust's first conservation area. Unknown to most people the little church by the roadside honours the name of Cromwell. Within are tombs containing the mortal remains of the Cromwell family including Henry, the best of Oliver Cromwell's sons who lived a mile away at Spinney farmhouse. After 1660 on the return of the Stuarts Henry lost his land and he decided to live a life of contentment as a farmer at Wicken.

During the Civil War Henry Cromwell became Lord Lieutenant of Ireland, and he held this position having succeeded his brother Richard who had succeeded his father as Lord Protector. Henry was a man of strong character and sound judgment and regarded as refreshingly fitted in service to the nation. He became a captain under Lord General Fairfax and later served under his father, Oliver. At the age of 22 he became colonel and represented Ireland in the Barebones parliament. The abject poverty of the Irish people gave him much concern and he was entrusted to report on the progress of the new parliament there. The government was led by Henry's brother-in-law Lord Fleetwood, the husband of Bridget Cromwell, Henry's sister. The army in Ireland held sway in several ways and Henry believed it played too big a part in governance. He was appointed Commander-in-Chief of the army and advised the council in Ireland. Henry became very popular in Ireland and his father was impressed.

Henry Cromwell proposed that Ireland should have a more constitutional government but Parliamentary generals would not favour that suggestion. Their intransigence induced Henry to offer his resignation several times and his father agreed that Henry be appointed Lord Deputy. An Englishman he was well liked by the Irish people because of his honourable attitudes towards them. He was offered land in Ireland worth £1,500 annually but he said he could not accept it because "Ireland was poor." Carlyle truly stated that Henry Cromwell was "an honourable figure."

Henry was concerned when his father was invited to become king and urged him that such a position was unsuitable; it was, he said, "a gaudy feather in the hat of authority." It was suggested that known Royalist sympathisers be heavily taxed but that was rebuffed. Henry welcomed the decision to make his brother Richard Lord Protector after their father's death and he himself accepted the appointment of governor general of Ireland. He did not agree that the Stuarts be restored to the monarchy of England although his father had put this to Charles I placing England under constitutional authority and Charles had thought to the contrary which convinced Parliament that he could not be trusted and ultimately led to his execution.

When Richard was deposed as Lord Protector Henry decided it was time to retire and pursue a private life. Carlyle wrote "Henry did that in a very manful, simple and noble way," testifying to his conscientious considerate devotion to duty over his years in office. Henry lost his father's estate in England, valued at £2,000 per year but kept his estate in Ireland which he had purchased. This was worth about £650 per year, a not unreasonable income in his time.

After the restoration of the monarchy several influential Royalists endeavoured to exert vengeance on the Cromwells. Henry Cromwell retired to Wicken and died at the age of 46, praised by Carlyle as "a man of real insight, veracity and resolution, very fit for such service that had befallen him." As a young person Henry bore heavy responsibilities in a land that had for centuries suffered a spirit of rebellion. He confronted things with admirable public spirit enriched with a rare sense of independence and judgment which earned him the respect of England and Ireland. After his father he personally was welcomed as a fine statesman. The times in which he lived were indeed troubled and Henry Cromwell shone out as a rare man indeed.

It is fitting that he was laid to rest in a modest little church with none other than a simple monument. The thrill of history is felt at Wicken. The modern oak screen was added in our modern age in memory of him and his wife, Elizabeth. At the east end a floor slab honours Oliver Cromwell's sister Elizabeth, her body lowered into the vault in 1672. Beneath another grey stone reclines the remains of the Lord Protector's grandson who died in 1685. Other grandsons of Oliver were born at Wicken, William who died in the East Indies in 1662, and Richard brought here from London in 1687.

Apart from representatives of the famous name of Cromwell and two medieval brasses the church has little else to show. A famous Wicken inhabitant, Isaac Barrow lies in Poets' Corner, Westminster Abbey; his nephew was Isaac Newton's mentor. After the Restoration of the monarchy no-one wanted Oliver Cromwell's body to remain at the abbey and it was exhumed from the grave and his head exhibited on a spike. What a shame his body walled up it is said at a north country monastery was not brought to Wicken and buried near his family. Oliver's wife was reputed to be a fine cook and wrote a menu book. She is buried in the churchyard at Northborough, near Peterborough. Her husband's head was secretly buried in the grounds of Sidney Sussex college, Cambridge.

A Monarch That Could Not Be Trusted

A remarkable fact emerged in the differences between King Charles the First and Oliver Cromwell who was not entirely unfriendly towards him. If the King could have been trusted, even at that most difficult time, he might have been saved. Cromwell expressly said that he did not believe that no man could enjoy his possessions in peace, when the King had less rights. Cromwell was not unfriendly and had been visibly moved when he received the King's children. He was much afflicted by the pitiable nature of the gathering. It may surprise some to learn that the Lord Protector often saw the King and would walk with him and talked with him in the pleasant gardens and long galleries of Hampton Court palace at the risk of damaging his influence with the army. What befell the King could be blamed entirely on his concealed ambitions. He secretly held hopes from the Scottish people and when he joined them friendships lessened.

The King had promised to make Cromwell and Ireton, the Lord Protector's son-in-law, noblemen if they helped him to regain his influence. At the same time he wrote the Queen a letter telling her he intended using Cromwell for as long as it suited him, then hang him. The letter was intercepted by Parliament's agents. It had been sewn in a saddle en route to the Blue Boar in Holborn and from there it would be sent to Dover and transferred to a ship. It had been said that Cromwell wanted the King to escape abroad thereby getting rid of him without any more trouble and danger.

Cromwell had a great influence on the army, but some troops were mutinous against him and he found it necessary to have one man shot in front of his regiment as a warning to the rest. The King was eventually sent to Carisbroke castle on the Isle of Wight and he led a pretty free life at that place. While on the island he carried on a pretended treaty with Parliament and he was in reality a prisoner. He was prevented just in time from escaping to a ship sent by the Queen in France, lying off the island. Parliament voted it would have nothing more to do with the King who quietly planned to avenge himself on Cromwell and Parliament. He could not be trusted and in the end it was considered safer for the country to have him put to death.

In his innermost mind Oliver Cromwell recognised the country had a need for a king in a constitutional role. Royal prerogative would never again encroach upon political (Parliamentary) will. In his role as Lord Protector he made it abundantly clear that Royal monuments and tombs must not be defiled and that Westminster abbey, the Royal church, must not be desecrated in any way. He had hoped to achieve all this by re-installing the King upon the throne.

A Man For All Seasons – And Reasons

Problems with Ireland had existed for a long time, that country attracting invaders without much thought to resisting them. Prince Rupert, nephew of Charles the First cast inquisitive eyes upon Ireland and in Cromwell's mind it would be necessary to secure a quick victory and solve the Irish problem for good. However, the result of his plans probably contributed to later troubles. Cromwell laid siege to a number of Irish towns and his controversial victory at Drogheda led to a long-standing diversity of opinion fueling intense Anglo-Irish relations reaching into our own times. He had confronted the town with his formidable Ironsides and invited the Royalist garrison to surrender but this was turned down. Cromwell resolved to gain a quick victory, ordering his dogs of war into action. Several thousand people, mainly Royalists, were killed in the assault. Cromwell said he was doubtful that more than thirty defenders had escaped with their lives. As with all his victories he was convinced he received divine guidance giving him the means to destroy the garrison at Drogheda, but later he may have had thoughts about the bloodshed. In the following months when engaged against other Irish towns and garrisons, he was known to offer very generous terms were they to surrender. This is barely mentioned by critics biased towards the besieged. At Dunbar, Scotland, many of his soldiers suffered from bronchial maladies and it seemed Cromwell was in no position to launch attacks upon the Scottish men who had dug themselves in substantial trenches. In a religious frenzy, it is said, he ordered his men upon the trenches forcing the defenders into submission and taking no less than 10,000 prisoners.

Cromwell was convinced God had chosen him to lead England from the wretched depths into which it had fallen. For him it was a golden opportunity to fulfill the prophetic vision he experienced as a youth. The English Parliament riddled with corruption, squabbling and selfish ambition (where have we seen that before?) inspired his wrath and he determined to put a stop to it. The day came when he entered the House then in session with a troop of soldiers and shouted at the Speaker and Members words that should be emblazoned on the minds of every MP and member of the House of Lords: "Ye sordid prostitutes, have you not defiled this sacred place, and turned the Lord's temple into a den of thieves by your immoral principles and wicked practices? Ye have grown intolerably odious to the whole nation." His Ironsides cleared the chamber and seized the mace which Cromwell called a "bauble." His parting shot was "In the name of God, go."

Cromwell, a plainly dressed man with a disciplined air, was not a dictator, he spoke in plain terms and believed he was driven by divine inspiration. "I would not seek to set up that which Providence has destroyed and laid in the dust, and I would not build Jericho again," he wrote.

Compared with English Kings and Queens throughout history Cromwell proved to be an excellent head of State, urged by his instinctive political moderation and modest temperament. For centuries England had blundered on in a chaotic, uncertain light and he introduced stability to the nation, setting it on the road to create the greatest empire in the world, infusing inventiveness among nations and recognising that skills are not the sole prerogative of a single state. Cromwell overturned rules persisting in the past that had made Britain poorer, and opened the country to Jewish merchants who had been banned for hundreds of years, thereby boosting valuable financial links with other mercantile powers. The Lord Protector enabled British expertise to make its mark upon the world. He extended a welcome to hundreds of European Protestants persecuted in their homeland by Catholic authorities. Among the many trades in which they excelled was that of manufacturing fine cloth, establishing businesses at Canterbury, Norwich and London. Refugees introduced drainage techniques to the Fens where they set up colonies principally at Whittlesey and Thorney. Exempt from military service for several years they hired and purchased drained land and transformed the Fens into the country's most virile farmland.

After Cromwell had died the Protectorate, without a visioned leader, broke up and General George Monck, a military commander, invited King Charles the Second to return to the country from his place of exile. Instantly the Restoration of the Monarchy was welcomed but it re-introduced unrestrained indulgence in physical pleasures and waste and squander. It was not long before people openly wished Cromwell held the reigns of power again. In 1667 Samuel Pepys wrote that he was generously told by the Dutch ambassador, who was mindful of the trouncing of his country's navy on two occasions, "Cromwell was a great man who made himself feared on land and sea."

Cromwell's legacy remains to this day, the country's affairs promoted by Parliament, not by the monarchy, encouraging commercial development at home and abroad, with freedom of religious belief, nurturing of cultural standards and good principles and blessed with an energetic middle class. Cromwell, described by John Maidstone, his paymaster as "a large soul" with hardly any equal, gave us international greatness and transformed Britain into a respected, enterprising nation of great magnitude.

The Queen's Influence

Charles the First was a congenial man but he could not be trusted, especially in his negotiations with Parliament. His failure to adapt to the role of a Statesman drew him closer to the block. He was married to Henrietta Maria a French woman who had an immense influence upon him. The Puritans were so much in charge of Parliament and the English people, the majority Protestants, did not relish the idea of their King marrying Henrietta, an ardent Roman Catholic. Charles' obsession with extravagance and indifference to the country's inhabitants sowed the seeds of discontent and ultimately civil war.

Henrietta was only sixteen when she married Charles and his subjects were not too sure the marriage was a suitable thing for the nation. It was a genuine love match and strongly cemented, four children born to the couple. The queen was a lively person and loved extravagance and Charles supported her in every way possible lavishing upon her endless riches. Her catholicism influenced Charles and one ponders that the King became progressively sympathetic and supportive of the Queen's ambitions and less favourable with the Protestant cause, steadily allowing himself to be immersed into Roman Catholicism.

The King's greatest error was his perceived Catholic tendencies which played a major role leading to civil war. Henrietta did her utmost to raise troops in the Netherlands to fight Parliament helped by her eldest daughter's marriage to Elector Palatine. Letters flowed regularly from Henrietta to Charles, and she strongly encouraged him to square up to the enemy. Charles tried to oppose Cromwell who had often talked amicably with him, and he put a great deal of trust in the Royalist army but it was no match against Cromwell's Ironsides. With the exception of the first battle the King lost successive battles against the superbly trained and disciplined Parliamentarian army.

The Queen was distraught when her husband was captured and she secretly dispatched letters to him when he was imprisoned on the Isle of Wight. Charles was courageous to his last breath and always acted courteously to his enemies. Henrietta lived on for twenty years and was overjoyed to see her son, Charles the Second, succeed to the throne. Under Lord Protector Oliver Cromwell England rose spectacularly to be a great, innovative and formidable nation. Under Charles the Second it sank again to a depressing level. The Queen's influence upon a kindly but untrustworthy King was too much for the nation and it cost him his life.